L
I
F
E

V
I
E
W
S

Published by Creative Education
123 South Broad Street, Mankato, Minnesota 56001
Creative Education is an imprint of The Creative Company

Art direction by Rita Marshall; Production design by The Design Lab/Kathy Petelinsek
Photographs by KAC Productions (Greg Lasley, Peter Gottschling),
Mo Yung Productions (Mark Conlin, Tim Hellier)

Library of Congress Cataloging-in-Publication Data

George, Michael.
Antarctica : land of endless water / by Michael George.
p. cm. — (LifeViews)
ISBN 1-58341-025-2
1. Antarctica—Juvenile literature. [1. Antarctica.] I. Title. II. Series.
G863 .G46   2001
919.8'904—dc21   00-045169

First Edition

2   4   6   8   9   7   5   3   1

LAND OF ENDLESS WATER

ANTARCTICA

MICHAEL GEORGE

OF ALL THE PLANETS in the universe, Earth is the only one known to support **life**. Surrounded by an oxygen-rich atmosphere, caressed by warm sunshine, and bathed by ocean waters, the earth is inhabited by an abundance of plants and animals.

There is a place on Earth, however, where few creatures can survive. In this place, rushing streams and hot summer afternoons do not exist. The land is covered with ice and snow, and **temperatures** are far below freezing for most of the year. This place is the continent of Antarctica, the coldest, windiest, and harshest place on the planet. Yet even here, life asserts itself.

Antarctica's landscape is both beautiful and forbidding.

Antarctica is located at the bottom of the world. It covers the South Pole, the southernmost point on the planet. Antarctica is slightly larger than the United States and Mexico put together and is surrounded by water. The only way to reach it is by ship or plane, traveling south from the tip of South America, Africa, Australia, or New Zealand. Beyond these warm lands lie the cold waters of the Antarctic Ocean, dotted by a few lonely islands of rock. As one travels farther south, the temperature gets colder and colder. Close to Antarctica, there are no more islands—only great **icebergs** floating in the frigid sea. Ships must weave their way through these huge chunks of ice to reach the frozen continent.

Most of Antarctica's **coast** is locked in ice throughout the year. Two great bays, Ross Sea and Weddell Sea, are covered by a thick shelf of ice that rises hundreds of feet above the ocean surface. Inland, the ice may be as much as two miles (3.2 km) thick. If all of the ice and snow that cover Antarctica were to melt, the world's seas would rise about 250 feet (76 m).

The icebergs that drift in the Antarctic Ocean come in a variety of shapes and sizes. Icebergs, which can be hazardous to ships, are added to the ocean when they break off the ends of glaciers or ice sheets during warm months.

Among the few places in Antarctica that are not buried under thick sheets of snow and ice are the continent's tallest **mountains**. These rocky, treeless slopes rise forbiddingly above the ice. Antarctica's highest mountain, Vinson Massif, rises nearly 17,000 feet (5,182 m) above sea level in West Antarctica. East Antarctica also has ranges of high, snowless mountains, mostly near the coast. Mount Erebus, an active **volcano** on the eastern coast, occasionally spews ash and steam high into the air.

Seasons in Antarctica, and in the rest of the Southern Hemisphere, are the opposite of seasons in the Northern Hemisphere. Midsummer comes in December, while midwinter is in June. During the winter, Antarctica is the coldest place on Earth. The temperature may drop as low as 90° F below zero (–68° C). Although the frozen land receives very little annual precipitation, howling winds whip up old snow to produce blinding **blizzards**. Winds can blow up to 200 miles

Many people visualize Antarctica as a flat, unremarkable landscape of snow and ice. But the continent actually has a variety of geographic features, including a number of majestic mountains.

(322 km) per hour—as strong as the most violent hurricanes—making temperatures extremely dangerous.

Antarctica's harsh **climate** is a result of the earth's movement around the sun. Once each year, the earth makes a complete orbit, or circle, around the sun. As the planet makes this annual journey, it is always tilted. For half of the orbit, from March to September, the South Pole is tilted away from the sun. During this period, the sun never rises at the South Pole. Antarctica endures six months of cold, dark winter.

For the other half of the earth's orbit, from September to March, the South Pole is tilted toward the sun. During this period, the sun never sets at the South Pole. However, it merely hangs low above the horizon, so its **rays** are very weak and cannot melt the snow.

Scientists believe that the snow and ice on Antarctica have been accumulating for 20 million years. They also believe that Antarctica was once a very different place, with warmer temperatures, large plants, and a wider variety of wildlife. This belief is based on plant and animal **fossils** and pieces of petrified

Seals are perfectly adapted to life in Antarctica. Most seal species, including fur seals (top), congregate in large groups. Southern elephant seals (bottom) are huge, with males weighing as much as 8,000 pounds (3,635 kg).

wood that have been found there. Such findings support the theory that Antarctica used to be joined to the rest of the continents and began drifting south to its present location some 200 million years ago.

Covered by ice, battered by winds, and gripped by endless cold, the interior of Antarctica is a forbidding place to live. Even so, a few hardy creatures make their homes on the ice-covered continent. These are not polar bears, wolves, foxes, or other fur-bearing **mammals** that live in the north polar region. In Antarctica, there is not enough food to support such large animals. The only creatures that inhabit Antarctica's interior are insects such as tiny, wingless flies. These insects are active only during the summer, living in clumps of moss and **lichens** that grow on exposed rocks. Most die in the fall, but a few survive the winter and reproduce in the spring.

The warmest part of Antarctica, and the place with the most life, is the sea that surrounds the continent. Vast swarms of tiny **organisms** live in the water just off Antarctica's shores. One of the most important of these organisms is the krill—a

Plankton (top) and lichen (bottom) provide food for native animals.

bright red, shrimplike creature that is about two inches (5 cm) long. Billions of krill inhabit the Antarctic waters, providing food for larger animals such as fish, penguins, **seals**, and whales.

Penguins are the best-known of Antarctica's animals. Thousands of these comical-looking birds cover the continent's frozen coasts. Unlike most birds, penguins cannot fly. They spend most of their time swimming in the cold ocean water, searching for **krill** and fish to eat. They use their wings as flippers and steer with their legs. Penguins have a thick layer of body fat and dense feathers that keep them warm and dry, even in the coldest water.

The two kinds of penguins most commonly seen on the shores of Antarctica are emperors and Adélies. Emperor penguins, standing about three feet (91 cm) tall and weighing up to 100 pounds (45 kg), are the largest of all penguins. They breed, hatch, and raise their young on Antarctica's **ice shelves** during the winter and come ashore

Adélie and emperor penguins are the most common penguin species found along Antarctica's coastline. Other native species include gentoo (top) and chinstrap penguins (bottom).

only during the summer. Unlike other penguin species, emperors do not make nests on land. Instead, the newly laid **egg** is placed on the feet of the male parent penguin. Hunching down slightly, the male places a fold of warm abdominal skin over the egg. For the next two months, all of the males huddle together to keep themselves and their eggs warm, while all of the females feed in open water to the north. The females return as the eggs are about to hatch and take over care and feeding of the young while the males go in search of food.

The Adélie penguin is much smaller than the emperor, with adult Adélies standing only about 18 inches (46 cm) tall. Adélie penguins **breed** on the coasts of Antarctica. They build nests out of pebbles and raise their chicks during the short Antarctic summer. During that brief time, the parents teach their chicks how to swim, catch food, and avoid enemies.

The penguins' worst enemies include **skuas**, which are one of the few species of flying birds that live in Antarctica year-round. Scientists have seen these predators flying near the South Pole itself, where few other creatures ever venture.

Only the hardiest of birds can survive Antarctica's harsh climate. These include Adélie penguins (top), caracaras (left), wandering albatrosses (middle), and skuas (right).

Skuas are fierce, strong birds with four-foot (1.2 m) wingspans. They are known to swoop down on penguin nests and steal unhatched eggs. Skuas will also fly away with penguin chicks if the chicks are left unguarded.

Penguins and skuas live in Antarctica year-round, but a few other types of birds migrate to Antarctica during the continent's summer season. Among these visitors is the amazing arctic tern, which makes the longest annual **migration** of any living creature. These long-distance travelers nest in northern Canada between June and August. When cold fall temperatures come to the North, the birds fly 11,000 miles (17,700 km) to summer in Antarctica. Other birds that migrate to Antarctica include the wandering **albatross**, the snow petrel, the cape pigeon, and the giant fulmar.

Small sea creatures and birds are not the only animals that live around Antarctica. The largest animal in the world—the blue whale—also lives in the waters surrounding the continent.

Antarctica's wildlife includes arctic terns (top), known for their lengthy migrations to the southern continent, and humpback whales (bottom), which can reach a length of more than 52 feet (16 m).

This giant mammal, which can reach up to 112 feet (34 m) in length, is twice as big as the largest **dinosaur** that ever lived. When it comes to the surface of the ocean to breathe through its two blowholes (the nostrils on top of its head), it sends a spout of water vapor almost 30 feet (9 m) into the air. Like most **whales**, the blue whale feeds only on tiny plants and animals filtered from seawater. The Antarctic Ocean is inhabited by a variety of other whales as well, including fin, humpback, killer, and sperm whales.

Seals also live in the seas around Antarctica. Like whales, seals are mammals and need to breathe air. When the ocean is covered by ice, seals make breathing holes by gnawing on the ice or bashing it with their heads. Most seals eat fish or krill. The ferocious **leopard seal**, however, hunts penguins and will even attack other seals, such as Ross, Weddell, elephant, and crabeater seals.

The only other creatures that live in Antarctica are humans, but this is a rather new development. Unlike the other six continents, Antarctica does not have a native human

Seals and birds make up much of the animal life in and around Antarctica. Among them are such species as southern elephant seals, fur seals, macaroni and gentoo penguins, and several types of albatrosses.

population; no people lived there thousands of years ago. Scientific exploration of Antarctica began just a century ago.

In 1901, several countries sent **expeditions** to Antarctica to study the weather, the earth's magnetism, and the southern seas. One of these groups was led by British explorer Robert Scott. A decade later, Scott led four men on an expedition to the South Pole, racing to arrive before a rival group led by Norwegian explorer Roald Amundsen. Scott used ponies to haul supplies. Unable to adjust to the weather as Amundsen's husky dogs did, the ponies died, and Scott's men were forced to carry their own supplies. When they reached the South Pole in January 1912, they saw the Norwegian flag, planted by Amundsen's party a month earlier. Plagued by misfortune, cold, disease, and hunger, all of the men in Scott's group died on their return trip.

In the place where adventurers once struggled for survival, some people now make their homes. Today, more than 4,000 people live in Antarctica

Skuas are the sole inhabitants in many parts of Antarctica, but human settlements also dot the coastline in certain areas. These settlements include old whaling stations (right and left), farmsteads (middle), and scientific stations.

during the summer, and more than 1,000 brave the winter months. These people reside in 43 towns called **stations**. One of these is the Amundsen-Scott South Pole Station, a scientific base named in honor of the rival expeditions. Stations in Antarctica are not like towns in the rest of the world. The people who live there must bring with them all of the supplies and food that they need. Even the materials needed to build the shelters must be transported by ships or planes from thousands of miles away.

Most of the people who live in Antarctica are scientists. They study Antarctica's history, climate, and wildlife, as well as the southern oceans. They come from many different countries, including the former Soviet Union, the United States, Canada, Japan, and Australia. Although many nations have established scientific bases in Antarctica, the continent is a **neutral land**—it does not belong to any country. Even as it slowly reveals its frozen secrets, the barren yet beautiful landscape of Antarctica remains free of human boundaries, as it has since the beginning of time.

Like humans, albatrosses in Antarctica prefer to live on the coasts.

SALTWATER'S FREEZING POINT

Freshwater, the kind of water found in most lakes and rivers, freezes when the temperature is 32° F (0° C) or colder. But saltwater, the kind of water found in the ocean, has a lower freezing point. Here is an experiment that will allow you to see for yourself how saltwater resists freezing.

You Will Need

- Water
- A measuring cup and teaspoon
- Two freezer-safe containers
- Salt
- A freezer thermometer (if available)

Preparing the Water

1. Set your freezer to its coldest setting (be sure to get permission first).
2. Measure out one cup (250 ml) of water and pour it into one of the containers.
3. Measure out another cup (250 ml) of water and pour it into the other container. Then measure out two teaspoons (10 ml) of salt and stir it into the water in the second container.
4. Set both containers in the freezer, making note of which one is which.

Observation

Check on the containers every 15 minutes. You will find that the water without salt will freeze first. Note how much longer it takes the salty water in the second container to freeze. When the salty water does start to freeze, use the thermometer to take its temperature. You'll find that it requires a freezing point considerably lower than that of freshwater. When you are finished with the experiment, be sure to return the freezer to its normal setting.

The freeze-resistant properties of salt help most of the ocean's water—even that around such icy-cold regions as Antarctica—to stay open throughout the year. It is also the reason that people put salt on icy roads during the winter. The salt works against the ice, melting it and making the roads less slippery.

CALCULATING TEMPERATURES

Scientists from countries around the world travel to Antarctica to study its weather and temperatures. But not all scientists use the same terms to describe temperatures. People from the United States measure temperatures using mostly the Fahrenheit (F) scale, and people from most other parts of the world use the Celsius (C) scale. To be able to put any temperature reading into terms that you can understand, you must convert it to the scale with which you're familiar.

To convert a Fahrenheit reading into a Celsius one, follow these steps:

1. subtract 32 from the Fahrenheit temperature
2. multiply the new number by 5
3. divide the result by 9

To convert a Celsius reading into a Fahrenheit one, follow these steps:

1. multiply the Celsius temperature by 9
2. divide the new number by 5
3. add 32 to the result

LEARN MORE ABOUT ANTARCTICA

The Antarctic Connection
P.O. Box 538
Jackson, NH 03846
http://www.antarcticconnection.com/

The Antarctica Project
1630 Connecticut Avenue NW
3rd Floor
Washington, DC 20009
http://www.asoc.org/

Glacier
(Online resource for information about
Antarctica)
http://www.glacier.rice.edu/

The New South Polar Times
(Internet newsletter written by the staff
of the Amundsen-Scott South Pole Station)
http://205.174.118.254/nspt/home.htm

The New Zealand Antarctic Institute
Antarctica New Zealand
Private Bag 4745
Christchurch, New Zealand
http://www.antarcticanz.govt.nz/

United States Antarctic Program
Raytheon Polar Services
61 Inverness Drive East, Suite 300
Englewood, CO 80112
http://www.polar.org/

Virtual Antarctica
(Virtual expedition of Antarctica on the
Internet)
http://www.terraquest.com/va/index.html

INDEX

Antarctica is one of the last truly wild regions on Earth.